# @dr.am.a_queen

A friend that saves her from boredom,

Activates her teen- female hormones; she felt they could build their own kingdom.

She can't blame her teen self for believing she got a future with a number on her phone that leaves a mere picture.

For insisting on following the trend.

For fantasizing on what isn't; walking the thread.

For believing that she needs him, something more colourful than valentine red.

For trailing his every word when they on the phone but in reality she avoids eye contacts with her playful ted

You made me put the salt in the fridge

And you kept the matchbox in a pot

I tried to escape the house but you locked it

I went right, found myself going the opposite.

@ dr.a.m.a_queen

I crumbled with the wall when I triggered the
flames  that got me burned and my feelings
disabled.

Like devoured palatables which sought to be
treated less of a tasty vegetable

My heart ran from rest, my lethargied
attention seeking arrest

My days became saddened gay that my
instincts scrutinized every being

Reminding me of my shame in freckled scars
that hid as part of my stretch marks

it scrawled my hate and promises to never
trust a soul, Again.

@dr.a.m.a_queer

Travel ahead to feed life to my past, and blind my
desires to refill their faith
Because my world is here

Erase the horrors and the doom, and exhale my fears to
ease my tears
Because my world is here

Writing is hard! tear more sheaves and refill the ink
Because my world is here

@dr.a.m.a_queen

She rode on winds of music, stealing my
perfections, relieving my aches.

 Her smiles and gait bore prints on the trees and
filtered the sunlight through leaves of memories, I
lived as I child.

She fed me tasty hope in her anger and a peace
which only the past craved.

I savoured the past that lingered in her presence.

Stay with me, I confessed

To knot the restless tides, as her gaze held my
feet.

Stay I say when silence replayed in our memories

She blinked my fantasies to life, and unlocked my
demons

Though we have nothing in common, her incivility
played minions connecting us

I choked on the colours that wafts from her, my
heart raced

@dr.a.m.a_queen

For she was life and more.

To knot the restless tides, as her gaze held my feet.

Stay I say when silence replayed in our memories

She blinked my fantasies to life, and unlocked my demons

Though we have nothing in common, her incivility played minions connecting us

I choked on the colours that wafts from her, my heart raced

For she was life and more.

@dr.a.m.a_queen

She rode on winds of music,
Stealing my perfections, relieving my aches

Her smiles and gait bore prints on the trees
And filtered the sunlight through leaves of memories, I
lived as I child.

She fed me tasty hope in her anger and a peace which
only the past craved.

I savoured the past that lingered in her presence.

Stay with me, I confessed

@dr.a.m.a_queer

I want the sexy in his croaky
voice

And the doggy nose above his
squinted eyes that twitches in
disgust to foul breaths that cursed his
every step, as the floor squealed
to his praise.

All the attention he got, is what I
crave and

The passion tinted in his soul
aganist incipient dismays

The thought of how noble he
was, in his flapping robe
overwhelmed my hopes as he
spoke in refined romance

Hinting at my hinges. Also, his
sincere sarcasm, I wanted

But not him

@dr.a.m.a_queen

Sometimes, I believe them
when they say, 'the only
thing I'm close to, are
books. If it had wings, it
would leave me too'

@dr.a.m.a_queen

When taste are blind
I'd see you more
The way you smile
Elated my heart, tickled
my shadow
I'd spill my emotions as

My heart sings a different
love note
A new song, cause we're
synced to one beat

Maybe I know nothing of love
Maybe my scars bleed from my
eyes of white pretense
Maybe I should keep shut and
be gone
But if this isn't love, what am I
hurting from

If I
See failure as a trait immune to
any success that thrusts to my
reach

That I saluts with a heavy wave
of happy
Would you see through my
barren

@dr.a.m.a_queen

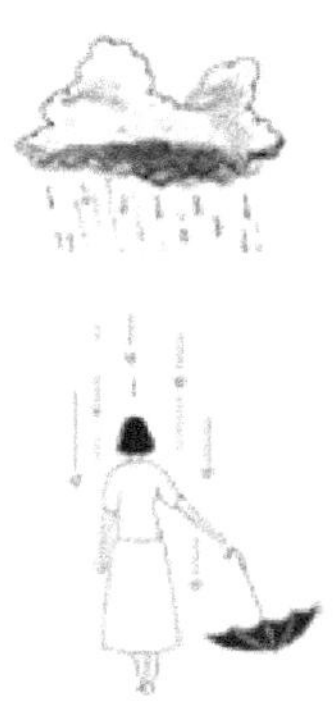

If I
Shut my lungs, letting my soul
escape me
But be called by my sons

For that's a relief, lest i be
thrown to the sands to bury
myself, their disgust sing i'm
weak

If I
Clean the sewers with my skin,
steal meat to be full
And I'm called psyche
Let to wander about
But the little one does it, and
he's not called anything

Cause his hope of growing is let
to die with the burning tyres on
his withered skin

@dr.a.m.a_queen

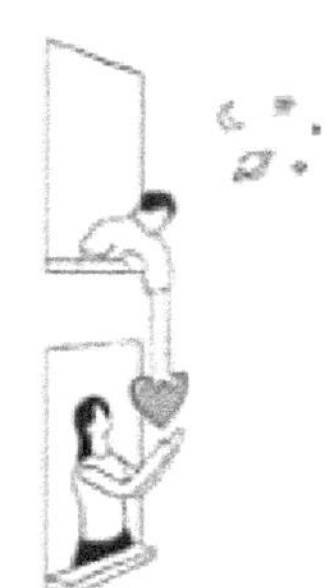

If I
Wear a new skin, tongue and
name
To stand in a wobbly fame as
your dame,
So fancy to be called Mrs
Chidubem
But racism isn't cured, rather
it's spoken plain

@dr.a.m.a_queen

If I command the gun
And be called dark
But he wears a gorier cloak in
stark
Twist of terse death, but he'd
be commended as a guy that's
tough

@dr.a.m.a_queen

Smooth whisphers love in my ears

The sky shares its smile in glows of lightning

I'm glad I'm doing this with you

Warm chills fill my cheeks as you kiss me shut

I closed my eyes til my fantasies close in

Drifting rustled leaves through my flying twigs

A light peeked in to my sight in lined rays

Trapping my pains and aches,

In a travel with the rest of you that wrecked me

@dr.a.m.a_queen

Strangle the ropes, delve in to
spooky hopes, I reach in
To blike the drama in our
storyline that'll be worth living
for;
A touch electrifying our
extremeties that steams fear
amidst

Breaking the hold and bond,
Over and over, we retry a dead
fate.

@dr.a.m.a_queen

Walk in my ghost
Steal my busy, occupy my
slack
With memories we shared
the most

@drama_queen

Hard struggle to mollify hunger as he is forced to
embrace the deathly truth

Growing the dear goods that soothe not the youths

Tripping the bridge, palliative stolen by hoodlums

The headline reads in to welled stomachs of nothing,
blaring twists of looms

O cheer old heart to choke than breathe

In air inspired to mortify lungs and suffocates dreams
underneath.

drama_queenservice
x

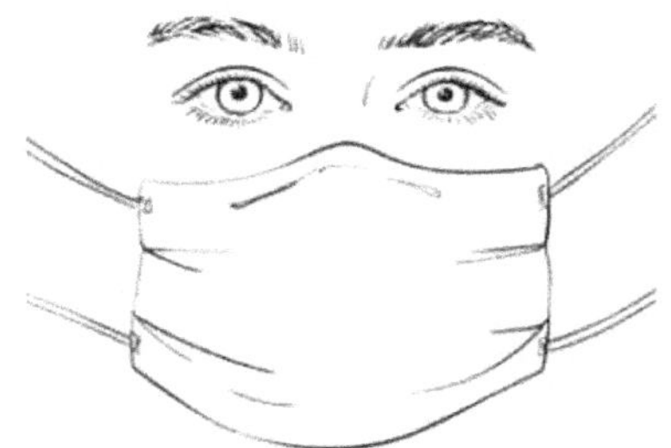

I live life slow

A life before time

But yearn for a love as fast

As my heart beats for you

dr.a.m.a_queenservics

# "THE HAVE NOTS"

Take a quick dive to the remote places they're tucked

They begged and hawked

Stomachs knotted with hunger

Where foods are out of reach.

When the population won't be enough

Would you tend their existence more than just food

when you intend to give,

Let your message be clear than the sizeable chumps

Shot in to depths of love to the have nots

@dr.a.m.a_queenservices

# "THE HAVE NOTS"

A cup or two
Two packs and few grains
Do I see a smirk of ingratitude, you dare not.
All they did was for the good of the have nots.

For a ball of akara, you did share lots
Not as rich as us, they did deserve the fair cut
The universe is pulling away from the greed
That wrecks not the eminent but

The desserted grounds hidden in fair huts
From  the eyes of empty.
Feeding nothing became a shared thought

@dr.a.m.a_queenservices

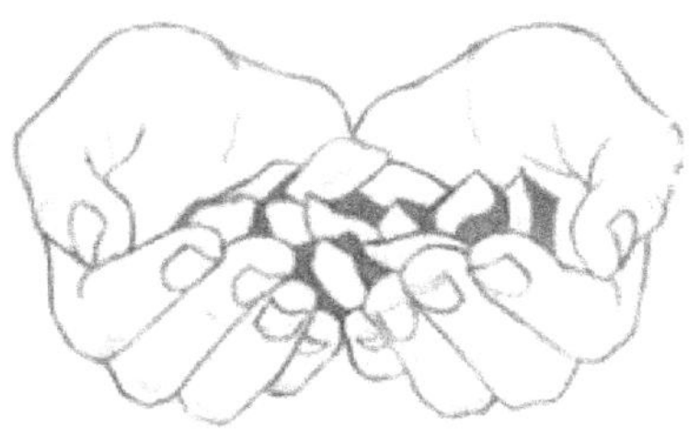

Your reactions will be withheld
by their voices
Their fingers will point at you,
Echoes of laughter telling you,
You'd never be like them.
Then you will break out,
Exclaiming what shouldn't be
said,
Again in a whispher, curses will
be sprout

She shouts and yells

A word from her, fills up
the rage

Steams more pain til you're
pale

Because she is your all,
your anger you cage

Silence killed you before
you could bail

Souls whose dreams

And hopes are drenched

In the broken soil


Why do we shoot

When no gun saluts

Her looks questioned my audacity
I neglected the formality in her tone

She spoke as if she wanted less to
partake in my company.

To the spewed words that wrecked
my eternity,
was the brief words she said

That I was too young for her

My forever love has left me
With words which weren't his
Whom I crave but his absence is all I shut
in